YOUR AMERICAN BIRTHRIGHT

INVESTING IN OIL AND GAS

by
Stephen M. Thompson

TABLE OF CONTENTS

FOREWORD

I was first introduced to the oil and gas industry in 1976. With an Honorable Discharge in my back pocket compliments of Uncle Sam's Marine Corp., I had tried my hand—somewhat successfully—at the Health & Fitness Industry. While owning and operating two fitness centers in Phoenix, Arizona, I was offered a business consulting contract by a small oil and gas firm out of Dallas, Texas. What started as a short-term project opened my eyes to a world of excitement and opportunity I had never imagined.

For the large majority of countries in the world, the natural and energy resource wealth of that nation state is the province of the very powerful, political, and privileged. Not so here in the United States! With tax benefits and direct access, every U.S. citizen has, in one way or another, the right and the privilege to participate and pursue commercial development of our country's natural oil and gas resources. Although not without risk, the opportunities available today are bigger and better then ever! Pursuit of the development of oil and natural gas is a privilege as well as a unique path toward profit and wealth building.

My hat is off to all professionals in all aspects of this industry that I have had the privilege to get to know and often work with. Thanks and enjoy the read!

Stephen M. Thompson

An Increase in World Demand

Over the last fifteen years, the impact of globalization has spread like wildfire, breaking past geographical boundaries and integrating humanity across varied levels of economics, politics, and even culture. Across the world, we are witnessing an outpouring of goods, services, and labor the likes of which has deepened bonds in just about every aspect of human life. Today, it would be nearly impossible for any single country to exist as a lone entity, cut off from any dependence upon other nations. To cut oneself off would be crippling. The fabric of most nations has been wound so tightly together that any major disruption would negatively impact the very foundations of society.

All the world's various cultures have, in some way or another, begun to gravitate toward the concepts pertaining to the free market. Given all the recent technological advances, most notably in telecommunications, it is not difficult to stay connected. Through the years, as our capacity to communicate has increased ferociously, so has the popularity of the free market.

As more and more people become beneficiaries of the free market, we find that the prices of commodities only keep getting higher. This is especially true when the commodities in question actually fuel the free market, leading it firmly down the long, winding road of human progress.

A culture without a free market is a place in which the people are not granted the opportunity to go about improving their lives. The building of schools and hospitals becomes nonexistent; the owning of a car or a home becomes virtually impossible. It is only when a free market exists that a push toward progress, structure, and independence can take place. And the basis for such a push lies in energy resources. Whenever and wherever energy resources are implemented, advancement and growth are ensured, and people are encouraged to take a step toward improving their lives.

With all this in mind, it is fairly easy to see how the market for energy consumption has expanded. Countries like China and India have significantly contributed to this.

In China, the rising middle class is just beginning to bridge the gap between the rich and the poor, making for a much broader-based economy. The central government in China has always encouraged the growth of science and technology, nurturing advancements and opportunities at every turn. As for India, its economy is on a gigantic upswing, touching upon a multitude of sectors as it carves out its own position as an emerging superpower.

As both China and India have reached superior economic positions in the recent years, they have started to compete with the U.S. for access to energy reserves. Up until 1992, China was in the business of exporting oil. Since then, it has gone toe-to-toe with the U.S. as a net importer of oil. Its consumption knows no boundaries; it is hooked in deep to the world market that generates this product every day. Currently, China imports an impressive 6 to 9 million barrels of oil daily, which does not even include the amount of natural gas being generated. At present, the U.S. and China combined are importing over 15 million barrels of oil every day.

Given numbers like these, it is not surprising to see that the world's demand for oil and natural gas is coming close to exceeding supply. Some predict that in our lifetime we will see the day when oil sells at $100(+) per barrel. As the demand puts a firm squeeze on those prices, the sky is the limit. Considering the fact that these resources are finite, prices will only continue to soar.

The world's population, now at about 6 billion, is predicted to increase to higher than 7 billion by the year 2020. With that increase, the demand for our natural resources will continue to grow, and we will find ourselves grappling with various solutions for how to press forward. In fact, we already are.

We are working to increase the supply, moving forward, full-steam ahead, as the earth gets more crowded and the effects of globalization continue to flourish and spread. At present, as energy companies continue to research and develop new projects, drill new leases, and keep their output steady, there are countless opportunities for investors to take advantage of. These opportunities involve investing in commodities that exceed local and regional lines, the global value of which continues to soar as a result of the world's collective push for progress. As we learn to recognize exactly what is involved in finding success in energy-related investments, we see that the possibilities are endless.

PART ONE

HISTORY, OPPORTUNITY, AND ACTION

CHAPTER ONE

The Roots of Your Birthright

The History of the Oil and Gas Industry

A s U.S. citizens, we are unique in terms of our ability to access oil and gas ventures throughout the world. Scour the globe and you will not find another country that offers individuals the ability to invest in this wealth-building resource on limited capital.

As a citizen of the United States, you have the opportunity to be a **direct participant** in the development of oil and gas. You do not have to take the backseat by simply limiting your investments to energy-related stocks and bonds. The doors are wide open. You can step right in and become a partner—or a key player—taking an active stance in discovering and drilling for oil and gas.

Places like Mexico and the Middle East boast a great deal of oil reserves, but they offer no access to the likes of individual investors. Instead, the governments keep these natural resources tightly under their control. Given its many reserves, Canada does tend to offer individuals some opportunity on a limited basis. However, no other country offers limitless access with incentives to direct participation like the United States.

In many countries, drilling takes place on properties that are owned and controlled by wealthy families, powerful groups, or governments. These exclusive groups of people are going to be cautious about how they manage their wealth. Sharing their money and spreading it around are hardly top priorities for them. As U.S. citizens, we are quite fortunate to be able to participate in the outright development of oil and gas.

In 1920, legislation was passed that allowed the leasing of public land for oil and gas exploration and drilling. A good portion of the leases—the ones that were deemed geographically valuable—was auctioned off to the highest bidder. The remaining leases, which were determined to be of less value in the oil- and gas-producing sense, were available to whomever came in first to claim them. As the old saying goes, "The early bird gets the worm."

Yet, after awhile, the competitive spirit that this practice inspired in people became threatening. People would do anything they could to prevent the man next to them from getting to the lease first. Violence ensued in some cases, forcing the Bureau of Land Management to step in and restore order.

In 1959, the first-come, first-serve element of the program was eliminated, and a lottery was put in its place. Any U.S. citizen, twenty-one years of age or older, could apply for parcels of land that would surface via the lottery every month.

This system introduced a noncompetitive edge because it was based solely on "the luck of the draw." However, it was also unstable in some ways because there were cases in which it was nearly impossible that the winner would receive more value from the lease than the government had collected for it. Despite such discrepancies, the system continued to function for almost thirty years. That all came to a halt in 1987, when the Federal Onshore Oil and Gas Leasing Reform Act was passed.

Given the need to adjust to the ebb and flow of the marketplace, as well as the need to enable a healthy dose of competition, the auctioning of leases was brilliantly implemented. Via this system, people would have the opportunity to take matters into their own hands, bidding for parcels of land that reflected market-value prices.

Still in place today, the Reform Act has continued to perform wonderfully. It is a systematic monument of the opportunity that we, as U.S. citizens, can take advantage of, should we wish to seek it out. The sky is truly the limit because the chance to explore and develop a variety of leases is ours for the taking.

And as a bonus, doing so entitles us to–

Tax Benefits

When you become a direct participant in oil and gas drilling, you become involved in one of the most significant and long-term tax benefits virtually anywhere in the marketplace (with the exception of home ownership).

Generally, taxpayers can elect to deduct intangible drilling costs under Code Section 616. Excess intangible drilling costs may be a preference adjustment for alternative minimum tax purposes. Subject to limitations, depletion expense is allowed under Code Section 611 (generally 15 percent of income). Depletion expenses may also be an alternative minimum tax adjustment.

Too many sophisticated investors are unaware of these facts, yet they have been in existence for quite some time.

Moreover, unlike many other modes of investing that only offer benefits to individuals who suffer loss, direct participation programs extend tax benefits to the successful investors as well. Regardless of whether oil or gas is found, the amount of money that goes into initial drilling and testing costs qualifies as a complete write-off. If oil or gas is, in fact, recovered, the investor can take advantage of an 8–20 percent exemption (depletion allowance) from federal income taxes on the profit generated by the project.

Of course, one does not get into an investment just for the sake of having a tax shelter. Years ago, there were volumes of complex multiple tax shelters available. These tax schemes, if you will, were attractive, as people in that era found themselves paying 60, 70, and even 80 percent in personal income tax. People were wasting all kinds of money, not caring about the deals they were getting themselves into. As long as they were getting tax benefits out of them, they were content. That is definitely not an intelligent way to manage your financial profile if you expect to experience any kind of significant growth over the long term.

In any direct participation program, the goal is to make money. It is to profit. It is to get ahead of the game while enjoying, of course, the 60–80 percent worth of tax benefits as secondary benefits.

<hr />

What drives the obsession with and the need for oil and gas? Why has the U.S. government been so quick to jump on this energy-related bandwagon, offering tax incentives, benefits, lotteries, land auctions, and direct participation in drilling and exploration programs? Perhaps it has something to do with the foundations of our country and its historical attitudes about progress, creativity, and abundance. One cannot understand the present without comprehending the past, so it is important that we examine the roots of the opportunity under discussion. Fortunately for all of us, it is quite a story.

The History

From way back in modern human history, using oil has always been the best way to keep fires lit. Heating and cooking were done with the likes of coal and wood, while basic illumination relied upon whale oil. This oil, taken from the nose of the sperm whale, burned with less smoke and odor than most fuels, making it extremely popular. It was so popular that the sperm whale was in danger of becoming extinct.

Eventually things shifted. As the Industrial Revolution kicked in, the world turned its attention away from whales, and fuel was needed to run generators and engines. The search for a new energy source was on. In the midst of it, a great discovery was made: kerosene.

Extracted from crude oil, kerosene could be used effectively as a light and heating fuel. The smell was less offensive than animal fuels, and more importantly, it was cheap and easy to produce. Its significance in the world economy started to gain some momentum at this point, and the petroleum industry began its un-precedented growth.

The First Wells

The first oil well in the United States was drilled in 1859. From a very shallow depth of 69 feet, Colonel Edwin Drake of Titusville, Pennsylvania, produced about twenty-five barrels of oil in one day. While that event marked the beginning of the oil and gas industry in the U.S., the world was hardly a stranger to it.

The first oil wells were drilled in fourth-century China. Using bamboo poles as their method for drilling, the Chinese could successfully achieve about 800 feet of depth! In order to do so, drilling bits would be inserted into bamboo, which was hollowed out, creating a "pipe," and reached far down to pull the oil and/or gas up to the surface. Over time, the Chinese had developed a system by which bamboo pipelines connected wells to salt springs, allowing for oil to flow much more efficiently than before. Through the centuries that followed, oil was steadily used to keep fires lit, and when 1853 came around, the process of oil distillation was discovered, revolutionizing the industry.

A Polish scientist by the name of Ignacy Lukasiewicz had figured out how to distill crude oil into kerosene. After this, in 1861, the first Russian refinery was built in the oil fields of Baku, which was producing almost 90 percent of the world's oil at that time.

Through most of the 1800s, it seemed that the industry was still trying to gain its footing. It was growing slowly, primarily as a function of people's need to keep their lamps lit. Everything progressed, however, after Colonel Drake's success in 1859. With Drake's discovery, people were driven to dig up more wells, and by the winter of 1860, the excitement grew as more and more depths were successfully ventured.

Barrels

After Drake's great discovery in the 1860s, the men in surrounding towns hit the ground running. As wells sprang up left and right, an issue arose regarding what to hold the oil in. Locations everywhere were ransacked, and the search for any kind of container was on. These men used whatever they found that could do the trick—beer barrels, whiskey barrels, containers of any and every type—as they rushed to take advantage of the fantastic opportunity.

Finally, as barrels started being produced solely for the oil trade, a standard size of 42 gallons emerged. This number was taken from King Edward IV in 1482. To maintain control over the packaging of fish, which was big business during that time, a statute deemed it necessary to package fish at 42 gallons a barrel. This size barrel remains the standard today.

The Fever

The oil fever was catching on. People across the country were trying their luck; with dollar signs in their eyes, they set out to match the success of Colonel Drake. Amid this craze, inevitably, the seed of investment was planted, and it took no time at all to blossom into a swelling industry that involved pooling money for the purpose of drilling for oil and gas.

Here's how it worked: A promoter would attain a specific lease and raise funds from friends, partners, and investors. Once he had all the money together, he would go and drill a well on the leased property.

This investment process continues mostly unchanged today. Both the nineteenth and twentieth centuries saw flourishing development and discovery with regard to the oil and gas industry. As a result, we now benefit from a natural resource that accounts for two-fifths of the world's energy needs. (The other three-fifths are accounted for by nuclear energy, solar energy, wind power, hydro-electric power, coal, and tidal power.)

The Giants of Today

People like John D. Rockefeller knew a hot opportunity when they saw one. Always one who was quick to jump on any deal he deemed worthwhile, Rockefeller's ears perked up when he learned of Drake's success. Without wasting a moment, he invested in a Cleveland oil refinery. Less than a year later, Rockefeller created Standard Oil, which, within a decade, was producing 95 percent of the oil in the United States.

All of this came to an end, however, when in 1911 the Supreme Court declared Standard Oil a monopoly that restrained trade. Standard Oil was then divided into thirty-four separate companies that were encouraged to compete with one another. Some of the giants of today were formed. Our country saw the births of companies like Mobil, Chevron, and Esso (renamed Exxon later on).

These giants grew larger as the auto industry swept the nation, raising the demand for gasoline refined from oil. With the ongoing need to locate new reserves, the exploration for and development of oil and gas continued with no end in sight.

CHAPTER TWO

Seize Your Birthright

A certain segment of today's world understands the importance of building a nest egg. It is the only way to get ahead and pull yourself away from relying completely on your paychecks. You want to be able to do the things you want day-to-day, right? With the finer things in life in mind, you invest. You take risks. You delve into stocks, bonds, real estate, antiquities, precious metals, collectibles, and whatever else may suit your fancy. And in the midst of it all, perhaps, **you make room for oil and gas investments because you understand the incredible benefits that they have to offer.**

Access

These benefits do not merely pertain to taxes. For starters, oil and gas investors are also graced with the gift of close proximity to the source of their investment. Stated simply, such investors are only a few phone calls away from the actual people that are manning their holdings. If there are any questions at any time, one can always pick up the phone or march directly over to the physical operations.

This is not necessarily so with various equities or financial instruments. If you have ever invested in stocks and bonds and have tried to reach someone of authority, someone with decision-making capabilities, on the phone, then you are aware of the difficulties this entails. Typically, when attempting such phone calls, you will end up a dozen layers (and a whole lot of hold time) away from the source of your investment.

For example, imagine that you decide to go ahead and make an investment with an independent energy company. Your company rep is on the phone with you. The rep mentions offhand that you are going to be getting paid $58 per barrel of oil. However, that is not the case upon arrival of your first check. Disappointed, you discover that you are only getting paid $52 a barrel.

Still clinging to the notion of receiving $58 per barrel, you are in need of some answers. So you get back on the phone with your representative, who then connects you with corporate. You call corporate headquarters, and after that, you're right on the line with **the company who actually purchased the oil.** With just a few mere phone calls, the answers are at hand and simple.

A substantial amount of comfort resides in this fact. After all, that is the way it should be. No investor should have to jump through hoops to get some information, especially after laying out serious and hard-earned money.

Later in this book, as we take a look at other kinds of investments, you will find that they all take you further and further away from the actual source. Things like stocks, bonds, and mutual funds put you many, many phone calls away from the heart of your initial investment. Answers do not come as readily. It is more difficult to keep track of what exactly is happening and, most importantly, *why* it's happening.

In the oil and gas business, with the right professionals, you have the ability to stay on top of your investment. You can track the progress of the drilling process. Pick up the phone and find out what transpired out in the field that week. The amount of comfort and control present in these kinds of opportunities truly makes involvement worthwhile.

Vitality

Moreover, there is something to be said for contributing to the exploration of commodities that are so essential to our progress and survival. Here in America, as the world's highest consumer of oil per capita, we have based a great deal of our day-to-day lives upon mobility and electricity. Given the depleting supply of reserves, it is incredibly important that we pursue the exploration of oil and gas on a variety of fronts, as doing so preserves the independence of our country. Without oil and gas, we would certainly not be free to do the things we would like to and enjoy the same quality of life, and until we come up with viable economic alternatives, we must continue to nurture the development of these resources.

Returns

Above all else, there is also the authentic possibility of high returns. When you are a direct participant in an oil and gas venture, you have the potential to make serious returns—**from 10 to 20 to 25 percent annually.** In some cases, 30 percent returns are reasonable expectations as well. Given the high numbers involved, the benefits are indisputable. Investments as advantageous as direct participation programs are unique and can, in the right hands, offer great rewards.

Act with Urgency

If you do not have holdings in the energy sector, you would be wise to get them **now.** Allow for energy-related opportunities in your investment portfolio. The high potential returns, the tremendous tax benefits—these are the things that will aid you in your quest toward financial freedom. As you set out to achieve these things, be prudent. Refrain from allowing slick marketing alone to dictate your decision-making. Do not be fooled by the new oil and gas company that comes onto the scene with their stock at thirty-eight cents and then next week, all of a sudden, sees their stock jump to eleven dollars. Do your homework. Find people you learn to trust and ask questions. The energy sector is going to be making quite a bit of money for people in these next few years, and if you want to ride that wave, equip yourself.

Regarding risk, Aristotle once said, "First, have a definite, clear practical idea. Second, have the necessary means to achieve your ends; wisdom, money, materials, and methods. Third, adjust all your means to that end."

Well put. Face risk with intelligent ferocity. Get all those ducks in a row before you plow ahead. Then do so because you are confident that rewards and success will be yours for the taking.

Direct Participation in a Nutshell

There is always a great benefit to availing oneself of the bigger picture. Do this, and all of a sudden your world is open to various options and avenues, as possibilities reveal themselves from dozens of directions.

The possibilities that come along with involvement in direct participation programs can be tremendous. You may find that the financial rewards from such deals seem to go on and on. *Sometimes, they actu-*

ally do. There are cases in which partners continue to receive decent returns on projects they acquired **twenty-five to thirty years ago.**

No doubt, this is an ideal state of affairs. We all want that, don't we? We are all looking for that cushion of financial freedom, right? We want freedom and independence. Regardless of the kind of lifestyle, most of us live up to what our incomes allow . . . and then some. The ability to enjoy our leisure time, our vacations, our hobbies—all this is greatly enhanced by financial freedom. It is about having your money work directly for you, as opposed to you working for your money.

That is one reason **developmental drilling programs** can be a key.

When you get involved in a developmental drilling oil and gas project, you are entering a world where the risk is kept to a minimum. In a developmental drilling program, you can breathe because you have the assurance of past success to guide you and the percentages are stacked heavily in your favor.

In a developmental drilling project, due to the fact that previous wells have proved successful, plans are made to resume drilling in the same vicinity. The odds tilt in your favor. Confidence is instilled. Risk is minimized.

If a given project has resulted in four very profitable wells and plans are made to drill another hole right in the middle of the four, then the outlook for success on this fifth well is fairly bright. Now, while nothing is ever 100 percent certain, the chances of success as a commercial well are certainly higher than if there had not been proven, profitable wells in the area. Developmental drilling is ideal when it comes to limiting the level of risk. Chances of success are increased, and with that, we move just a little closer toward financial independence.

In May 2006, Bolivian president Evo Morales took the drastic action of deciding to nationalize the oil and gas in his country. Accordingly, he instructed his military to occupy all of Bolivia's oil and gas fields.

Should they stay on with Bolivia, foreign investors will not be receiving the profits that they have been contracted for and agreed to. Morales has given them a six-month deadline to sign a new, revised contract— one that would damage each company's profits tremendously. By taking this action, Morales has closed off an avenue of the free market that will most likely prove disastrous to his country's economy in the years to come. It is very possible that other South American countries will follow suit, turning the tide further and further away from democratization and free markets in the process. Places like Venezuela and Ecuador have already taken measures to this effect. In Venezuela, revisions to contracts have been demanded, giving foreign investors less stable footing in their energy-related projects. In addition, Ecuador recently took control of an oil company that was U.S.-operated. With the government controlling natural resources in this way, global opportunities are drastically limited, and the chance of spurring worldwide progress via energy investments is compromised.

Fortunately, such is not the case in the United States. The government we have is rooted in democratization and respects the capital markets. Its foundation was built to encourage its citizens toward greater possibilities by promoting the ideals that deem economic participation and financial involvement worthy pursuits. Americans can stake their own claims. Our financial independence helps us press toward the future with great resourcefulness. The benefits that come with direct participation oil and gas ventures have the power to bring us closer to the things that we want most. *Seizing those things is our birthright.*

CHAPTER THREE

Three Kinds of Wells

The Good, the Bad, and the Ugly

In the early days, as reserves were being extracted, high science was not the order of the day. There was no sophisticated technology that aided in the quest for the extraction of oil and gas. In its early and adolescent stages, the industry had it rough. It was a long, drawn-out process that lent itself heavily to inefficiency.

As an example, somebody would take the wheel off the back of his truck. He'd go find a belt, then attach it to that wheel. After this, he would go out and get a tool that he had used in the past for digging water wells. Using this contraption, he would be able to venture down about 300 feet. If he was lucky enough, he would soon find oil making its way out of the ground, eventually lining his pockets in the process.

Fortunately for that person, he did not need a great deal of money to get access to fancy equipment. Because such equipment did not exist, he had to essentially make do with what he had. The downside was that he would not be able to ever hit the depths that we have become accustomed to hitting in the present. Though we certainly pay the price with the many thousands of dollars it takes to do intensive drilling, we are able to get more out of the ground than ever before. **That is, of course, if we are able to locate reserves.**

Locating Reserves

The greatest reserves untapped today are offshore and/or in volatile areas. Not only that, but offshore drilling and hostile environments can be tricky and dangerous. These reserves are far from the market and can be of lesser quality, making them more expensive to extract and refine.

So much of our supply comes from volatile parts of the world, and of course, we do not necessarily play well with all of them. Though we trade with folks in the Middle East, a state of war exists, and it shows no signs of vanishing any time soon. These commodities that we rely upon so intensely are in the hands of producers that are not friendly to our interests. We have to be delicate in handling our dealings with them. Some major politics come in to play here as well, but that's a whole other book entirely. Stated briefly, as compromised as these relationships may be, the economic future of our nation is highly dependent upon them. It also brings added value and necessity to domestic production.

The Good: Successful Wells

In any oil and gas venture, risk can be minimized in numerous ways. At the outset, the investor's major concern is the simple preservation of capital. For an investor, finding oneself in the same position one was in when one started is far more desirable than taking a loss.

So, what is the easiest, most practical way that you can minimize your investment risk and come out with **the good**—the successful commercial well? Simply stated, you hire the best you possibly can. You arm yourself with contractors who have proven themselves out in the field. You research and evaluate until you have found partners with the required know-how and expertise.

From my own experience in the oil and gas industry, I can easily attribute a great deal of my success to strong relationships formed over the years. Such relationships can ensure a higher possibility of future successes.

Moreover, one should find out all the answers to all the pertinent questions:

What's the company's track record?
Who are the principals of the company?
How long have they been in the business?

By surrounding yourself with the right people, you can minimize the risks that accompany your investments. Nine times out of ten, when you approach independents with the kinds of questions listed, they will be eager to invite partners in for a piece of the action on a lease they are preparing to drill. If, after stomping around on the field and doing all the appropriate research, it is determined that there are viable, proven reserves, it is then time to seal the deal.

If you do your research, you can find the team that will take you to the top. Ideally, that team will be composed of a group of experienced individuals, all with the skill to get the job done as efficiently as possible. Before you sign on with a given company, be certain to check all the facts. If you have the opportunity to drop in and take a look at the lease with your own eyes, take advantage of it. You must be able to justify having faith that these people will do the absolute best they can with your investment interests.

Needless to say, it is unwise to pass your investment off to just anybody. The process of locating and drilling a well can get very complicated, so it would behoove you to align yourself with professionals who are experienced and well-suited to handle problems or difficulties that may arise. Once you hire the company that you feel is best-suited for the job, these professionals will engage in an intricate process, bringing them closer and closer to getting the drilling started and to the possibility of a commercial well in the process.

When you are looking for an attractive lease, it must be noted that **location is everything**. You need to have a good place to start; otherwise you really have nothing. The lease is the foundation of the entire project. It must be studied, examined, subsurfaced, geology reviewed, and evaluated until the probability of an underlying commercial well is determined to be exceptionally high. Going about it any other way would not make for a successful venture.

To fully determine the value of a lease, a good amount of information must be gathered. Research and evaluation cannot be taken lightly. Hundreds of thousands, many times millions, of dollars are at stake. A new series of pertinent questions must be asked:

Does the lease come with an operator or without?

Are there transmission lines?

Is there access to market?

All the blanks must be filled in before you determine whether or not it is worthwhile to engage in some drilling.

Now, once the team has a specific lease in mind and all the evaluation has showed some promising results, it is on to the drilling phase. But before that happens, it is necessary to secure the right to drill from the owner of the land. Sometimes that owner will hold all interest in the land; other times his or her interest is just specific to the mineral rights. When a contractor is acquiring the right to drill, it usually involves leasing the oil, gas, and mineral rights of the property. A "lease bonus" is arranged, and the owner receives a substantial cash bonus in exchange for extending the right to drill, extract, and sell the oil and/or gas.

Additionally, there is the matter of royalties. No matter what comes up and out of that hole, the owner will retain a piece of the pie, as long as it is part of his or her leased land. The amount of the cut always varies, and sometimes, unfortunately, holes turn up dry and the owner comes out of it with no royalties at all. The owner does not share in any of the production costs. They are the responsibility of whomever holds the right to drill and develop the lease.

The royalty held on property by a landowner will usually fall somewhere between 12.5 percent and 17.5 percent. The percentage range does fluctuate. In today's market, it is not unusual to find 17.5 percent to 25 percent royalty demands. This is especially true with leases in valuable, prime areas, places in which lease after lease has proven successful. Of course, if you own the land, you understand the great potential that your area has to offer, so why give it up for too low of a price? Years ago, many owners would settle for just

12.5 percent without a second thought, but things are no longer what they were. As landowners take notice of the success of those around them and become aware of the demand's exceeding the actual supply, they are motivated to put a higher premium on their holdings, demanding higher royalty percentages.

The Bad: Unsuccessful Wells

If you do decide to venture out on oil and gas programs, you may find that things take twice as long to get done as you initially thought they would. Production problems, equipment failures, and even contract disputes can occur, sometimes bringing the project to a halt. Count on these little "surprises" to manifest themselves at the most inopportune times. These things will happen. Just remember: Very seldom does anything turn out as you thought it would. Let this be your mantra, and you will make it through the process with your sanity intact as you prepare yourself for the unexpected.

When negative circumstances find their way into the mix, assess the situation with an undiluted, level head. *It is not the worst that could possibly happen.* If you ask me, I would rather have a delay in production than come out with a dry hole as the end result. A dry hole is a dead-end. Once you come up empty, it is over for that round. The well is plugged and abandoned. Its value now lies in tax benefits and useful information, which will aid in evaluating the next drilling location. So keep things in perspective, and do not be deterred by delays or an occasional dry hole.

Since we are discussing unsuccessful wells, it seems fitting that we go into the possibility of losing a well, whether it be due to a dry hole or to human or technical error.

There are no guarantees in life. You can drill ninety-nine successful commercial wells in a row, and on that hundredth one, things can go wrong. Equipment failure, human error, and sometimes just plain bad luck may lead to your bidding that well *adieu*. Of course, the crew works hard to ensure that the equipment will be operating properly at all times, but the unforeseeable may emerge at some point, regardless of all the meticulous planning and experience.

As has been explained, if I drill four commercial wells, and decide to drill the fifth one right in the middle, the odds of hitting a fifth commercial (successful) well are extremely high. But nothing can ever be taken for granted, as certain as we may be in a situation like this one. Accordingly, the professionals are still necessary. The testing is still put into action. Proof must be acquired in order to propel us to put the finances into the drilling. Even in the face of great certainty, we must evaluate and interpret information in order to substantiate our beliefs and goals.

As the process evolves, it is fundamentally prudent to make the informed decisions and align yourself with the most qualified, experienced professionals. The alternative to that will only result in loss of time, as well as capital.

The Ugly: Misrepresented and Mismanaged Wells

Two of the worst problems you can encounter are ignorance and negligence. The damage they do can lead to insurmountable obstacles. This means that basic tasks or day-to-day operations will not be run properly, leaving room for any number of errors to occur or problems to go unchecked.

A poor team can (and will) lose a well, eliminating or putting an end to monthly revenues. Any number of situations can occur. If the team slouches the least bit toward inefficiency, equipment can be lost in a hole and become impossible to retrieve. If this occurs, the hole must be plugged and abandoned.

You must protect your investment. Your money is going into paying people to be competent and to take care of business to the best of their ability. If they are not doing their jobs properly, what could very well be a profitable program ends up going south.

Title work is a part of the process that is just as important as drilling. If a title is not properly secured in the beginning, you may find yourself in an undesirable position. However, it is a lucky day for the farmer or the individual who owns the land. He will be thrilled beyond belief, having just received a free well that is entirely his! He has no responsibility whatsoever to share it with anybody. When this occurs, hundreds of thousands of dollars could go right down the drain. As controllable as it may seem, some deals have fallen through due to a lack of proper title. But when you have the right legal people in place, situations like this are not likely to occur.

Of course, as with anything, natural problems can occur. When it comes to the mechanics of drilling, a wide variety of activities takes place. Truth be told, a drill site can be a tricky and dangerous environment. It may not be like working on a fishing boat in the North Sea, but it can have its moments. And the more hostile the environment, the higher the degree of danger. Working on a rig is probably one of the most dangerous jobs in the world. There are a lot of moving parts involved. Numerous people are working onsite, operating heavy-duty machinery, which can lead to unfortunate accidents.

Moreover, there are characters in every industry, characters who can really end up costing you by misrepresenting what they can really do for you. Jumping onboard without doing the research and asking the questions may land you in a situation where you invest a great deal of money only to find that an unprofitable well has been drilled. Perhaps the people you signed on with did not really gather all the necessary facts to evaluate the situation. They may be novices, just recently setting foot in the industry, and you have ultimately become their guinea pig. That is why a company's track record is important in determining whether or not they have what it takes to securely handle your investment dollars. On the flip side of all this, there are also people of the highest integrity who will "guess wrong" from time to time. This potentiality must be understood in the context of any business deal.

With all this in mind, realize that most things that can go wrong are not insurmountable. Solutions can be created. Work with a good team, and oftentimes actions can be taken to remedy the most negative of situations.

CHAPTER FOUR

The Drilling Process

There are three core facets to the oil and gas industry. Each one is categorized according to its place in the "stream." The first one, the "upstream," pertains to the exploration, production, and processing of crude oil and natural gas. The "midstream" pertains to the pipelines and tankers that bring crude oil to refineries and natural gas to gathering systems and distribution points. The third facet is the "downstream," which pertains to the refining, marketing, and retail leg of the industry. Gas stations are included in this third category.

The residue left behind from organic waste is what leads to the creation of hydrocarbons. This waste can generally be found on the ocean floors, originating from land plants and microscopic plankton. Naturally abundant in carbon and hydrogen atoms, this matter collects itself in porous sedimentary rocks over millions of years. When the matter is converted into hydrocarbons, oil and natural gas form. From here, the pressure and underground heat cook everything up, and once this occurs, disruptions in the rock's layers create pockets that capture the oil and gas, sealing droplets thereof in between permeable rocks.

When an exploration is mounted in search of these hydrocarbons, it is essential to find a good source of layers of rock beneath the surface of the earth. But the question is: how does the explorer identify a potential source?

The Right Characteristics

The formation of a rock is incredibly significant. If a rock does not have porosity, then the odds of extracting commercial quantities are simply not favorable. Pores effectively allow glimpses into the measure of the openings in a rock, and it is in these openings that the hydrocarbons may be found.

Permeability is another important factor. Without it, the pores of a rock would not be connected, which would not allow for the hydrocarbons to move freely (or "migrate") from pore to pore. Without such connectedness, the chances of producing oil decrease greatly. Pores without any permeability are nothing but a useless venture: there would be no means by which your oil or gas could flow successfully into a well.

Equally important is the presence of some kind of trap, which is necessary to prevent the petroleum from leaking away. These are either stratigraphic traps or structural traps. A stratigraphic trap is present when the bed of the reservoir finds itself sealed off. This occurs when a layer of the permeable rock is cut into, stunted by another rock that is impermeable. Sometimes a stratigraphic trap can be found when the bed of permeable rock is simply enclosed by impermeable rock.

Structural traps, classified as either a fault trap or an anticline, come into fruition when a disturbance, a kind of deformity in the petroleum-filled rock, prohibits movement of the petroleum.

Whatever the trap may be, it absolutely must be located in order to ensure the collection of oil.

Now, even with these characteristics in check, exploring for oil can be a fairly complicated process. In

all the many years that these hydrocarbons were coming into formation, events occurring in the crust of the
earth were constantly shifting things around. For one
thing, earthquakes would cause some major cracks
within the crust. Even wind and water erosion were
factors, exposing and then burying certain formations.
Over the years, a number of factors have interfered
with the Earth's temperament, causing oil and natural
gas to shift around and journey away from the place
from which it originally emerged.

Some of the oil deposits managed to make it to the
surface (collecting into pools of tar). But as the chang-
ing tides of the Earth pushed the petroleum upward,
some of it was not so successful in plunging ahead to
the top. Instead, it was pushed back by impermeable
layers of rock and held far, far underground.

How We Search

Presently, there are quite a few more steps in the search
for oil and gas than in previous times. For instance,
cultures like the ancient Chinese found product by just
hoping that a good source was nearby when they came
upon oil seeps. As advanced as they were at the time,

their approach to the complicated world of oil or gas exploration was very basic.

Today, geologists are needed to examine the rocks, and if these rocks are not exposed in surface outcrops or by core sample, satellite images and aerial photos are the next best thing. Seismic geologists also come in handy here, poring over geophysical data in order to gain insight into valuable conclusions. Shockwaves are sent into the ground to determine the amount of time it takes certain rocks to refract the waves right back to the surface. The geophones that measure this process provide the data that computers then process and convert into seismic lines. These lines can then be used to create three-dimensional computer models of the rocks and their intricate underground geometries.

All this science is of great value, but in the end, the drilling has to begin in order to know what truly lies beneath. When actually drilling a well, all kinds of data become available. These are the data that will end all speculation. These are the data that will (finally) uncover the gleaming truth, leading to the answers necessary to determine whether or not to complete or plug and abandon. If the data look favorable, the well will be completed as a commercial producer. If not, the well is plugged and abandoned, and it's on to the next location.

With today's sophisticated technology allowing industry professionals to see what is happening deep below the earth's surface, potential success in exploration has been substantially improved. The importance of accuracy is not to be underestimated. Drilling a well is costly; take as much of the guesswork out of the project as you can (and never discount "good luck").

Ready to Drill

Once the preliminary details are locked down, the crew can immerse themselves in the project. They labor to clear and level the land, sometimes building access roads for convenience. Then a few holes are dug to make way for the main hole and the rig. Also, a pit is dug right around the drilling hole; this pit will serve as a catch-all for the cuttings from drilling activity.

Once this is all completed, actually beginning the business of going for "pay dirt," surface casing is established according to the state's criteria, to seal off and prevent any contamination of freshwater or other natural resources. With this all done, things can really progress.

Rotary drilling is a process that consists of creating a hole through the continuous turning of a significantly important tool called the bit. Extremely heavy in weight, the bit is attached to the drill stem, which includes hollow pipes that lead to the very top of the derrick. The bit is key, serving as the end of the drill that cuts up all the rock with which it comes in contact underground. The rest of the rig, which includes the derrick and attendant machinery, is designed to ensure that the bit is always working at its absolute maximum capacity.

Drilling fluid, referred to as mud, is a prepared mixture of clay, water, and various chemicals and weighting material. Part of the circulation system, this mud is purified and recycled, as it moves down the drill pipe and through the bit, eventually leading out to a surface pit.

This fluid is vital in a multitude of ways, one of which has to do with its ability to remove hole cuttings without needing to remove the bit. As a result of this ability, the process can unfold in a straightforward, timely, and efficient manner. Upon being moved upward by the mud, the cuttings provide highly effective data to study for determining the presence of oil or natural gas. On top of that, the mud is useful for lubricating the bit in the hole, and also preventing a blowout, which could occur if the bit ever came across a high pressure formation.

Equally noteworthy (and some feel more efficient) are air rigs, which adhere to the same overriding principles as mud rigs but use air as the means of removing hole cuttings.

Ready, Set, Drill

A competent, experienced crew knows firsthand the ways in which patience and preparation make for successful results. No professional in this industry can afford to waste money (or time) by rushing in on a job and losing it due to some error that could have been prevented. To be sure, bad things can happen regardless of the amount of preparation, but as previously mentioned, minimize the risk in any way that you can. Because the work out in the field is so particular, you will need to surround yourself with a diligent team that boasts a track record of past success.

With the utmost precision and patience, your crew will now determine a preset depth, which will lead to the drilling of a surface hole. Ranging anywhere from several hundred to many thousands of feet, this depth is a determined point, referred to as the "total depth." Once it is hit, if hydrocarbons are present, the possibility of a successful well is on its way to becoming a reality. All through the drilling process, formation cuttings are brought to the surface by the mud (or air) and the producing formation will be revealed, bringing the testing part of the process carefully into action.

Testing

In the process of well logging, a logging company arrives, lowering gas and electrical sensors to the very bottom of the hole. Once this is complete, the devices are methodically pulled back up to the surface, making measurements and recordings of rock formations and data as they pass by them.

These sensors are able to produce a record or a graph, which is studied to determine whether or not oil or gas is, in fact, present in commercial quantities.

Coring, which involves taking various samples of rock to study for certain characteristics of reservoir rock, can also aid in facilitating the process. This is usually accomplished by assembling a core barrel, which is run into the bottom of the hole by way of a drill string. The barrel rotates, and upon doing so, cuts an actual core in the shape of a small cylinder, which is then studied. Drill-stem testing is also a useful tool for determining the presence of reservoir rock, by way of a device being lowered into the hole to specifically measure the pressures.

This is a crucial point. Other than confirmation by sight or smell, the information generated by the well logs will dictate whether or not completion is called for. If the results prove unsatisfactory, then we are faced with what is referred to in this industry as a dry hole. But if, after studying every bit of relevant information that the formations in the hole can provide, the geologist can most certainly detect a significant presence of oil and gas, then the crew must get to work in completing the well and seeing through this mission.

Completing the Well

If substantial commercial production is to flourish, the deliverability of the product must be controlled. That is what transpires in the completion process. There are a number of ways to complete wells, and depending upon the location, depth, and pertinent information, the opinions on how to accomplish this will vary. Various treatments and completion procedures can be involved.

Treatments

Depending upon a number of variables, most wells will need to be "stimulated" to enhance or even induce the migration, or deliverability, of the oil or gas.

An action called acidizing can be used, if necessary. In a formation containing zones of low porosity, it becomes difficult for oil or gas to flow forcefully into a well. Through acidizing, this can be solved, so long as the formation is made up of rocks that react favorably when exposed to acid. Limestone reservoir rock is an example. Via acidizing, thousands of gallons of water-cut acid can be pumped down into the well, allowing for the acid to contact the formation. The crew continues to pump, pushing the fluid mixture deep into the formation, which allows for the carving of little channels through which the oil or gas can migrate in order to enter the well bore. Sand is used as a propping agent.

For a reservoir rock like sandstone, different measures must be taken to substitute for the lack of permeability. Through a process called fracturing, a specially-blended mixture of fluid, sand, and nitrogen foam is pumped down the well, contained and directed straight for the formation under extreme pressure. This fluid contains various materials, called proppants, which consist of things like walnut shells and sand. This special blend builds in pressure as the pumping continues, eventually fracturing the sandstone. These fractures will be necessary in allowing for the easy migration of oil or gas, and the proppants remain lodged in them to keep them open.

If, after all this, the well continues to perform below its potential, artificial-lift and/or vacuum equipment might be used to increase production. In a method known as "pumping," which involves rods and surface pumps, a pump is placed in the bore of the well, with a sucker-rod string attached. While pumping, a drawing or lifting occurs, which brings the oil up to the surface.

Initial production methods will produce primary recoverable reserves, which is precisely why *secondary recovery methods* are instrumental. However, uninterrupted initial production is ideal. Completed properly, initial production can last from a number of months to upward of thirty years.

Secondary Recovery

As oil is extracted, the pressure responsible for bringing it up into the well inevitably reduces. Secondary recovery, which sometimes involves the injection of substances (water or steam) into the reservoir, must be put into action to keep "pushing" the hydrocarbons to the well bore. In order to inject these substances, an injection well must be available. Once the injection well is in place and the agent is injected, the pressure exerted on the formation is increased, and the flow is stronger as it heads to the well bore.

In some situations, the oil may just be too thick, or "heavy," to flow. In this case, steam may be injected into the formation under high pressure. The heat that is produced causes the oil to thin, and with all the pressure, the oil can move swiftly to the well.

Waterflooding is another often-used and extremely efficient process of secondary recovery. The water is injected into the target reservoir in order to revive it and essentially "push" the hydrocarbons toward the well system. Once this action takes place, the water can really get in deep and bring the remaining oil up and out toward the wells. As the amount of oil heading outward decreases, more and more water will have to be produced. The flooding stops at the very moment that the oil coming up is no longer economically viable in proportion to how much time and money is being spent on the flooding.

In a lot of cases, it will take a few months to make any real headway in the flooding process. The entire process can last up to a decade, as it steadily produces oil. It is not surprising to see that you will gain some major ground within the second or third year of the process.

During the initial methods of recovery, it is usual to find that about 15 percent of the oil is recoverable. When finally incorporating waterflooding into the mix, it is safe to say that another 15 percent of the remaining oil will be recovered. After that, there will still be reserves left in the reservoir, but the means by which to recover them will not be worth pursuing economically. Today, technology continues to offer more and more options.

Wells, Wells, Wells

When a reservoir is found or a field is established, significant amounts of hydrocarbons, revenue, and profits are generated. Most operators prefer drilling a series of offset wells to the first hole, establishing the parameters for development. Before signing on to any oil and gas project, the sophisticated and savvy investor should always seek programs or operators whose past success can be pinpointed. Otherwise, why tread in uncertain waters? There is no reason to subject yourself to the pressures that uninformed investing can bring. In truth, the process can be exciting *if* you make the decision here and now to use the common sense and homework that lead people toward smart, financially viable opportunities.

When reviewing a lease, it is most desirable to see that a reservoir or field has been established. Stepping into the process any other way oftentimes means much too much risk, or "wildcatting" (see the glossary). At the very least, see to it that whoever you choose to participate with knows how to take action in an aggressive and sophisticated way—one that could take you toward your goals as a successful investor.

What Happens Next?

Upon being extracted, the hydrocarbons, or oil and gas, are ready to be sold. Things can turn a couple of different ways, depending upon the types of contracts and transportation arrangements. In most cases, all the participants (landowners, royalty owners, working interest partners, etc., etc.) enter into a contract with one buyer. The proper division of money through an assignment or division order is determined, and funds are distributed to everybody accordingly. Distribution of revenues is generally consistent as payment on from 30- to 90-day cycles.

If one wanted to crystallize the essence of this chapter, the breakdown would look something like this:

- **Find it**
- **Drill it**

- **Produce it**
- **Sell it**

The steps are as simple as that—simple but far from easy. These are the ideas that form the foundation upon which the oil and gas industry thrives. Perhaps, by seeing how simply it is expressed here, you will be able to turn visions into reality and pursue strong opportunities.

Your income will be the outgrowth of all the things that your investment provides to the global community. Your stake in the development of energy paves the way for a million other actions to unfold around the world.

The crude oil is sold to a refinery, where its chemical chains are separated and molded into a variety of different products. By way of distillation, these products begin to take shape and play useful roles in all facets of life.

Via oil refineries, a number of energy products are made possible. Suddenly, there is aviation fuel for jet engines. There is diesel fuel. There are motor oil, tar, waxes, asphalt, and gasoline. Here is just a partial list of the ways in which crude oil can be used:

- **Grease**
- **Lubricants**
- **Transportation fuel**
- **Cooking fuel**
- **Heating fuel**
- **Aviation fuel**
- **Motor oil**
- **Tar**
- **Waxes**
- **Asphalt**
- **Gasoline**

Though we may tend to take many of these things for granted, their impact on the quality of our lives is massive; it also supports the independence and freedom that our country has fought so hard to sustain.

Some people may see it the opposite way. It may occur to them that we are in a slave-like position and that we would be frozen in place if our oil suddenly ran out. The idea that we are functioning as slaves to oil is a tremendous misconception. Though decreasing supply is a real concern, we have used these commodities as a mode of empowerment, as a way to enrich the freedoms that we hold so dearly.

Find It, Drill It, Produce it, and Sell It
The Oil and Natural Gas Program flow chart

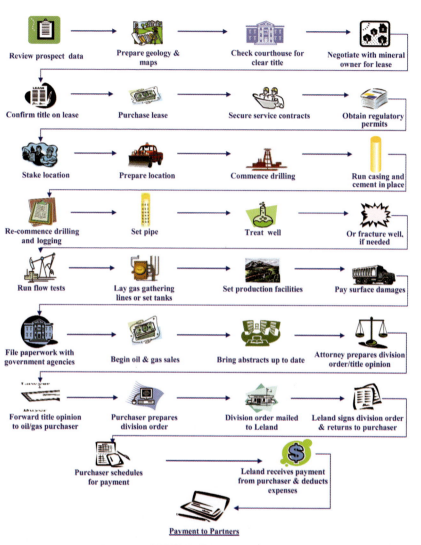

Drilling rig on site

Drilling activity, Knox County, Kentucky

Open flow of oil from an oil well

Tank being set on site

Oil pump jack on site

Oil storage tanks, Green County, Kentucky

Barrels of oil ready for pick-up by transporter

An open gas well, Knox County, Kentucky

Nitrogen fracturing process, Clay County, West Virginia

A flow-test on a gas well, Fentress County, Tennessee

Gas transmission line installation

Compressor station for gas transmission

Site reclamation and re-seeding

Gas well, meter box, and flow line

Gas meter and pipeline

Author reading pressure at the well head, West Virginia, 1976

30 years later in 2006, author still finds
the time to read pressure at the well
head during a field visit in Kentucky

PART TWO

ALTERNATIVES, RISKS, AND QUESTIONS

CHAPTER FIVE

The Lure of the Equities Market

Alternative Avenues in the Energy Sector

The equities market offers other avenues for those seeking involvement in the energy sector. It is not uncommon to wonder about the difference between stocks, bonds, and other investments and direct participation.

Stocks

The volatility of the stock market is commonly recognized. Without question, the presiding incentive of the investment banker or stock broker is to make money for the house. This is done through commissions and the sale of stock. Accordingly, there could be many incentives that motivate the typical investment advisor. Also, no person, no matter his or her cited level of expertise, can soundly predict the market's cycles.

Added to these volatile factors is simple numerical logic. The conventional stock market investor can anticipate annual returns, after winners and losers, of approximately 10 percent, as compared to the potential of higher returns and monthly revenue that can be had via direct participation programs. Finally, the aforementioned notion of *access* is not to be forgotten because the stock market investor is many more steps away from his or her investment than the direct participation partner.

Bonds

Part of the appeal of bonds lies in their comforting level of predictability. Additionally, because bonds are sold in small dollar amounts, those who invest in them need not fear parting with sizeable sums of money. Better still is the fact that bond prices are not generally prone to large fluctuations. The reliability of bonds gives them a rare standing among investors.

Notably, of course, bonds do not offer high returns. As for long-term bonds, they tend to be low-yielding as a result of rising interest rates. Already low yields can be further eroded by inflation. Accordingly, whereas security is a strong factor, gains can be limited.

Mutual Funds

The variety that is inherent in mutual funds exists to secure gains through diversification. However, the mutual fund investor plays no critical role in the placement of his or her funds. Such work is left to the fund's portfolio manager, which of course impinges upon one's own maneuverability.

In the meantime, *dilution* presents one of mutual funds' steepest downsides. Despite the principle of diversification operating within one's fund, the varying performances of the fund's components can result in inertia, generating fees but little actual net gain to the investor.

Options (Puts and Calls)

To be sure, the purchase of stock options seems appealing and productive, but they can carry higher risk.

When purchasing a put or a call, one must speculate and risk steep losses. Indeed, one has to be certain about a given asset's course, as well as when it will reach its expected destination.

Diversify with Knowledge

Because direct participation programs potentially can have high yield and monthly revenue, they are a uniquely intelligent investment option.

The purpose of this chapter is not to encourage readers to abandon their present portfolios but to illuminate direct participation programs (with regards to oil and gas) in contrast to other vehicles or financial instruments. Diversification is encouraged here, so long as the investor knows the nuances of his or her options.

CHAPTER SIX

Risk Issues

A s in any business, risk is always present. While it cannot be totally eliminated ("no risks, no rewards"), research, verification, and homework (if you will do it) can and will oftentimes prevent avoidable losses.

Larger-Scale Risk

Along with the many negative factors that can arise onsite, economic and political risks need to be taken into account.

In terms of economic risk, one must determine whether or not oil and gas will be produced at the current market value. If prices start to shift downward, what the investor originally expected to receive might, in the short term, prove disappointing.

Moreover, as we learned before when discussing Bolivia, Venezuela, and Ecuador, political interests are capable of disrupting matters. Fortunately, as citizens of the United States, we need not generally live in fear of a nationalization of resources that would directly impair our profits or earnings.

Minimizing Risk

Fearsome are the days when investors learn that their capital has vanished. Such is why it is important to avoid one-well programs. At a minimum, the oil and gas investor should aim to be involved in multiple-well programs, thus preserving strong odds. As we know, in developmental drilling programs, the odds of multiple wells helps secure the investment.

Walking Away

No feeling equals that of "bringing in a well." There are instances, however, when despite the classic indicators of looming success, problems can occur. Accordingly, it is important to know when to walk away.

Suppose a successful program hits four or five wells in a row. The owner of the lease could become greedy. Rather than charge $20,000 for a location, the owner may now decide to charge up to $100,000 per location.

Unless the operator is willing to negotiate, the best option may be to turn and walk away. Knowing what to do and when to do it is a fundamental aspect of ensuring long-term rewards and/or profits.

CHAPTER SEVEN

Frequently Asked Questions

Does investing in oil and gas qualify as a wise short-term investment?

When becoming a direct participant in an oil and gas project, it is best to always consider long-term strategy. Going into a project with a short-term mindset does not allow one the chance to authentically build and nurture an energy-related portfolio.

Does one require a sizeable amount of investment capital?

It takes money to make money. Typically, oil and gas ventures are offered to accredited investors. (These are individuals with a net worth of approximately $1 million, high annual income, etc., etc.) Not only should these individuals have a high level of liquidity, but they should possess a level of sophistication and the ability to properly evaluate information. Those with limited investment experience and capital should be extremely cautious and patient with themselves.

Explain how payment functions in a direct participation program.

If and when gas is brought up, it goes through a process of compression, transmission, and dehydration, is metered and measured, and is then sold to the PUC or the gas company. As it is extracted, it is constantly being fed into the line and sold. A graph charts the flow of gas out of the well every single minute of every single day. Checks are distributed in accordance with the recorded assignments and division orders.

In regard to oil, the process differs. A truck arrives to pick oil up, and once it does, a note or a "trip ticket" is left or sent, detailing how much oil was taken. Usually, within 30–45 days thereafter, a check is sent to the master lease holder or operator, and the aforementioned check distribution process unfolds.

Is there any noteworthy factor that could cause oil and gas prices to fall?

If one follows the pricing, one will see that the prices of oil and gas do still fluctuate considerably.

By way of an example, between late 2002 and throughout 2003, the base price for natural gas (its bottom) was between approximately $3.50 and $4.25. Two years ago, in 2004, that base price was up to between $4.24 and $5.50. In 2006, while we have seen $15.00 per mcf, $6.00 appears to be the bottom in the natural gas market.

It is essential to track a commodity's bottoms in order to fully determine the direction it is headed. One mustn't simply track those bottoms over a six-month period of time but over a two- to five-year span. Doing so will confirm that the consolidated base for natural gas and oil has continuously gone up. Given the peaks that bring the prices way up, the numbers probably will not recede to yesterday's levels, even when they fluctuate up and down.

Is it reasonable to expect the price of oil to reach $100 per barrel?

Twenty-five years ago, there was much discussion about that occurring, but the price never made it that high. Today it looks more likely. As of approximately August 2006, we had seen the price of oil reach over $72 per barrel, which is not that far from $100 per. Any number of world or market occurrences could push the price closer to the $100-per mark.

Is it reasonable to state that oil is significantly overpriced?

It is fairly safe to say that while there will be corrections in the market, the price of oil will continue to rise in the coming years. There will be no stopping the price of oil as it continues to rise in the coming years, especially here in the United States. With this in mind, however, it is worth noting that the price of oil remains a bargain. Upon attempting to price an entire barrel of cola, milk, or wine, one would find that those items cost substantially more than a barrel of oil.

The claim has been made that developmental drilling for natural gas and oil is the most limited-risk procedure in the area of direct participation. Is that true?

Developmental drilling means that a given party has already drilled and completed a number of wells on a particular lease. The rate of success for drilling commercial wells on such a lease tends to be excellent.

Is the use of natural gas exceeding that of oil?

In terms of domestic use, the future preference will consistently lean toward natural gas. It burns "clean," and we are developing it on American soil, which makes for a wealth of security and convenience. Since the late 1970s, most residential, commercial, and industrial use has been geared toward natural gas.

Oftentimes, when drilling, gas is hit prior to oil. Is it customary to hit gas and then stop? Or is extracting the oil pertinent?

Whatever is found, if found in commercial quantities, will be extracted and developed. If both are discovered, they will be produced dually.

Might one be advised to take part in "wildcatting" (see the glossary)?

If you have a tremendous appetite for risk and have boatloads of risk capital. Otherwise, there is no reason to take part in this method of exploration, given the available technology and research capacity for evaluating developmental wells.

When do people's brokers contact them regarding direct participation oil and gas programs?

Very, very seldom. For a number of reasons, investment houses, brokerage firms, and financial professionals lean toward more conventional financial products to offer their clients.

Carpe Diem / Seize the Day

With oil production peaking in many places throughout the world, every single country is on the lookout, jockeying for its own position, ferociously holding on to all of its valuable oil and gas.

At the turn of the last century, oil was being sold for only 5–8 cents per barrel. The excitement spread rapidly across the world, and many cultures started to adapt and take advantage of this resource.

After World War II, huge fields were being found in wide and varying locations. In particular, people were shocked by the number of wells that were being found in Libya. Libya was experiencing astronomical volumes— in the vicinity of 50,000 barrels per day. Meanwhile, in postwar California, multimillionaires were being made left and right. With all the new wells springing up, it seemed like the abundance would never end.

At this point in time, we all know otherwise. No newspapers are filling their front pages with stories about another Saudi Arabia or Libya being discovered. Indeed, there is still intensive research going on, to say nothing of the fact that we have come so far in developing sophisticated technology that has broadened our ability to find and recover these reserves. Demand, however, still is outpacing supply.

Overstating Reserves

Quite a few countries have fallen into the habit of overstating their reserves. This is not that odd or unusual. For the past ten years, the Middle East has notoriously published reserve reports that are received by industry professionals with skepticism.

Given the current political climate, the United States and the Middle East share a deep and mutual distrust. Accordingly, they have no choice but to put their best foot forward, keeping us wanting what it is that they have.

Needless to say, we cannot help but want it. The very growth of the United States and all other open societies hinges greatly upon our use of oil and natural gas. We are never going to get to the point where we have no use for transportation or factories.

The practice of overstatement serves as a barrier. There are nations that will not allow any audit whatsoever on their current reserves. Their evasiveness creates mystique; it gives them a terse form of leverage.

Meanwhile, another powerful incentive encourages oil-producing countries to keep their data under wraps. OPEC currently imposes on its members a maximum amount of oil that can be produced daily, basing the number on a portion of the remaining reserves that each country has stated. This works out well for each country that overstates its reserves, for even though they may not have access to as much reserves as they claim, they can maintain high output and continue to rake in strong dollars. It is no wonder that some of these nations exercise their right to refuse any type of audits.

Peak Theory

In the meantime, communities all around the world are growing larger with each passing year. This can only mean continued profitability for the energy sector.

This is not to say that economic cycles will not impact matters. Naturally, recessions will continually occur in various parts of the world. Factors such as war and natural, as well as manmade, disasters, which have been amply present in recent times, can and will affect pricing, and yet—if history has taught us anything—prices will always find their way up again.

However, we are wise to look ahead—twenty-five to fifty years down the road. There is discussion of the entire world hitting "peak oil," reaching the point where our valuable commodities are tapped out, leaving us in the worst possible position. The theory is that when our oil runs out, many of the simple luxuries in our lives will no longer be within reach.

A geologist named Marion King Hubbert formulated the theory regarding what we accept today as "Peak Oil." By studying the existence of current reserves, he found reason to believe that the United States would reach its peak in oil extraction by 1970. Furthermore, he believed that the rest of the world would peak thirty years later. Obviously, the defining precept of every peak is that once one is standing on top of it, one has to ultimately make a downward descent, no matter how long that may take.

In regard to our oil situation, this is not the best of news.

Hubbert was correct in one regard: Our oil production did peak in 1971. However, world production has not quite hit that mark, though some believe we could see it happening within the next fifty years.

Whenever an oil reserve is located, production starts out relatively small because studies are conducted before the drilling has begun. Over time, the presiding principals see to it that the area is brought up to a capacity that is conducive to the maximum extraction of oil or gas. As they do so, they inevitably reach a point at which the amount that they are extracting out of that hole reaches its absolute peak. From that moment onward, the product will start to dwindle, or deplete, until it tapers off and there is no more to extract.

There is also a period right before the oil runs out completely in which more energy is needed to extract and process a barrel of oil than the amount of energy that is within the barrel. This is the point at which Hubbert states it is only fitting to abandon the project, believing that the time and energy being put into the process is simply not worthwhile. After starting with this basic foundation, Hubbert was inspired to look at the *entire* picture of oil and gas and determine that large-scale events would transpire in an identical fashion.

The Ratio to Watch

In the middle of the nineteenth century, the production of oil and gas was primitive yet advancing. These were the times when fields were plentiful. Large fields were recovering approximately fifty barrels of oil for each barrel that was used in the extraction and refining process. Over time, as oil fields have been depleted with each passing year, this ratio has decreased dramatically.

Estimates have been formulated regarding how much of the world's reserves have been tapped. On average, it seems that 45 to 70 percent of the wells on this planet have been depleted. Of what is remaining, the Middle East is believed to have about 50 percent, making it the top contender for oil reserves in the world. At the present juncture, there is still a bit of uncertainty as to the amount of reserves that each country contains. This condition stretches back to the aforementioned habit of overstating oil reserves.

What To Do?

Undoubtedly, the entire world will hit peak oil in the future. Whether one is a conspiracy theorist or an open market theorist, one cannot soundly contend that there is plenty of oil and gas for indefinite world use.

Because demand is now exceeding supply, the prices will continue getting squeezed. **The world currently consumes more than three times the amount of oil and gas that is discovered.** Our challenge is going to be keeping up with this widening gap with each passing year. The rising population will not make this an effortless task.

A total of fifty-one producing countries have hit their peak in oil production, and six more as of October 2006 were currently on the brink. This means that they will produce a declining amount of oil year after year. They will simply start digging into their reserves, continuing to dip all the way down until . . . nothing.

Some Hope

That is the stark reality. Granted, we will not be without these commodities as early as tomorrow, but it is safe to say that the oil and gas industry should be looking to restructure itself within the next twenty-five to fifty years. If we want to maintain the healthy position that we find our country in, then we have to change with the tide. This involves delving into the realm of synthetic possibilities, taking aggressive action forward, and developing alternate energy sources.

In truth, a great deal is available to us. The sun is immeasurably powerful. Technology now allows us to reconfigure its energy so that we can source it.

The wind is another prime source that we have learned to harness. We now turn its power into electricity as a means of fueling our factories.

Hydrogen is another bountiful resource. With it, human beings can replace the combustible engine and rewire the future.

To accomplish the above, oil and gas companies will have to start modifying the ways in which they identify themselves. To embrace the needed shift to synthetics, they are going to have to start looking at themselves as Energy Companies (that is, if they wish to remain powerful contenders in the industry 100 years from now).

In his 2006 State of the Union Address, President George W. Bush stated that we are addicted to foreign oil. He expressed that the country has a need to start stretching out and becoming more independent. The very same thing was said in 1973 by then President Richard Nixon. He stated that by the end of the '80s, we would be completely independent and have no need whatsoever for foreign oil. Unfortunately, that never occurred. If we do not strive toward alternate forms of energy, we will have no chance of retaining the comfort and freedom that we take for granted presently.

Until that time, if we decide to become direct participants in oil and gas projects, we are not only strengthening our financial profiles but are contributing to the human push for progress. The opportunity is there for the taking. We have the ability to seize what is in front of us—to take full advantage of our birthright as U.S. citizens—and contribute to the overall abundance of the world we live in.

Carpe diem.

GLOSSARY

acidize v: to treat formations with acid as a means of increasing production.

artificial lift n: any method for raising oil to the surface once a well stops flowing.

bit n: the actual boring or cutting component used in drilling wells.

casing n: the steel pipe put in a well to prevent the walls of the hole from collapsing, prevent movement of fluids between formations, and support well control.

core n: a cylinder-shaped sample extracted from a formation for analysis by geologists.

crew n: 1. the team of workers on a rig. 2. a group of oilfield workers.

crude oil n: unrefined liquid petroleum that ranges in gravity from 9°API to 55°API and ranges in color from black to yellow.

cuttings pl n: the pieces of rock taken out via the bit and carried to the surface in drilling mud. Geologists analyze samples of cuttings to learn about the formations drilled below.

derrick n: a big structure used for load-bearing, often bolted together.

developmental drilling n: a process of drilling wells that limits risk. With repeated success in a given area, plans to drill future wells in close proximity are developed to ensure potential success.

diesel fuel n: a mixture of light hydrocarbon for use in diesel engines; the boiling range of kerosene is just below that of diesel fuel.

drill v: to bore an opening in the ground.

dry hole n: a well that fails to produce commercial quantities of oil and/or gas.

flowing well n: a well with its own oil- and/or gas-producing reservoir pressure, which is not dependent on artificial pressure.

fluid injection n: injection of liquids and/or gases to make oil move into a well.

mud n: the liquid that travels through the well bore during workover operations and rotary drilling.

oil n: a hydrocarbon mixture that, via refinery, can yield kerosene, gasoline, etc.

operator n: the proprietor, lessee, or other person or group that oversees the outright operation of a lease or well.

permeability n: a measurement of how easily (or not easily) a fluid can flow through the connected pores of a given formation.(The millidarcy is the unit of measurement.)

petroleum n: a solid, liquid, or gaseous naturally occurring substance consisting primarily of carbon and hydrogen compounds. When measuring oil and gas, petroleum only refers to liquid hydrocarbon oil rather than natural gas and the liquid forms thereof.

pump n: a device used for raising fluid to a higher level or increasing the pressure on a fluid.

reservoir n: a natural body storing oil and/or gas.

rig n: the draw works, derrick, and related surface equipment of a drilling unit.

rotary drilling n: a drilling method in which downward force is applied to a rotating bit while it drills a hole.

secondary recovery n: 1. the use of gas injection or water-flooding in maintaining formation pressure. 2. the process by which a depleted reservoir is treated with water-flooding.

well n: the hole formed in the earth via drilling.

well logging n: recording information that pertains to geologic formations at a subsurface level.

wildcat n: a well drilled optimistically despite the absence of surrounding oil and/or gas production.

ABOUT THE AUTHOR

Stephen M. Thompson is the president and CEO of Leland Energy, Inc. His more than 30 years of industry experience includes most aspects of the "oil patch" including field work and lease and contract negotiations, with a recent primary focus on developmental drilling activity in the Appalachian Basin. Over the years, additional drilling and lease acquisition activity in Texas, California, Oklahoma, and New Mexico has provided him with a wide range of contacts and experience in the exciting energy resource business.

He is an ardent advocate for increasing domestic production of oil and natural gas to lessen America's dependence on foreign product, and he travels around the nation leading professional discussions on the state of the energy industry.

Thompson also serves on various boards and volunteers his time and money to charitable organizations, primarily at-risk children groups. He is the proud father of four children and resides in Beverly Hills, California.